# Islamic finance:
practical efficiency and ethics

Finances publiques/Public finance

Les finances publiques connaissent un développement important et se diversifient. Cette discipline couvre notamment les finances de l'État, le droit public financier, le droit fiscal, les finances communautaires, les finances locales, les finances sociales, les finances internationales et comparées, les procédures fiscales ainsi que le droit douanier. Ces questions peuvent être envisagées dans un cadre national, communautaire ou mondial.

La présente collection a pour vocation de publier des travaux originaux (thèses, essais, colloques...) ou de facture plus classique (manuels, commentaires de textes, recueils de documents...).

Elle a aussi pour ambition de rééditer des ouvrages aujourd'hui introuvables, mais fort utiles, dès lors qu'ils s'imposent comme référence et qu'ils sont agrémentés d'une préface substantielle.

Public finance steadily developing and diversifying. This discipline more particulary covers state finance, public finance law, tax law, EU finance, local finance, social finance, international and comparative finance, tax procedures and customs law. Those questions can be considered within a national community or global framework.

The aim of this collection is to publish original works (theses, essays, symposiums...) or more traditional ones (textbooks text analyses, collections of documents ...).

In addition, it is meant to re-publish books which are currently untraceable no matter how useful provided they stand as genuine references and contain substantial prefaces.

Dernières parutions

Mounir AOMARI, *La bonne gouvernance des finances publiques au Maroc*
*à la lumière de la loi organique relative à la loi de finances*, 2025.

Alexandre NICOLIER, *Le risque professionnel et le droit fiscal*, 2024.

Jean GIARD, *Le système fiscal international : une construction conceptuelle et pragmatique*, 2024.

Oumarou Sanda Awal

# ISLAMIC FINANCE: PRACTICAL EFFICIENCY AND ETHICS

## Numerical case studies and comparative perspectives

L'Harmattan

5-7, rue de l'École-Polytechnique - 75005 Paris

www.editions-harmattan.fr

ISBN : 978-2-336-58778-3

EAN : 9782336587783

# 1. Preface

This book is the culmination of a journey that combines academic excellence with hands-on professional experience in the field of finance. Holding a Double Master's degree with Highest Honors from two of the most prestigious business schools in Germany and France, and recipient of the Friedrich Naumann Foundation Excellence Scholarship (Germany), I have always been driven by a pursuit of expertise and innovation.

With over fifteen years of experience as a consultant and manager for multinational companies such as Renault Sport F1, Air Liquide, L'Oréal, and Lazard Bank, I have had the privilege of contributing to strategic projects at the intersection of finance and digital transformation. These experiences have deepened my understanding of global economic dynamics and the challenges facing financial systems worldwide.

This book on Islamic finance goes beyond a purely theoretical exploration. It provides a comparative, practical, and data-driven perspective on the world's two major financial models: conventional finance and Islamic finance. Through real-world examples and accessible analyses, it demonstrates how Islamic finance, grounded in ethical and sustainable principles, can offer viable alternatives to today's pressing global challenges.

My ambition is to make this discipline accessible to all—whether professionals, students, or the simply curious—and to open a broader dialogue on the solutions it can bring to the global economy.

## 2. Introduction

The world of finance is undergoing a period of profound disruption, where conventional models—long regarded as unshakable—are increasingly being challenged. In this context, Islamic finance emerges as a relevant and necessary alternative, offering ethical and sustainable solutions to global financial challenges. This book seeks to provide an in-depth exploration of this model, comparing it with traditional systems while highlighting its relevance for modern businesses.

My academic and professional journey has enabled me to develop a unique perspective on these issues. Holding a Bachelor's degree in Finance with Honors and a Double Master's degree in Finance with Highest Honors from two of the most prestigious business schools in Germany and France, I had the opportunity to delve into the intricacies of international financial systems. I was also honored to receive the Friedrich Naumann Foundation Excellence Scholarship—an award reserved for an academic and social elite after a highly selective process. This recognition not only validated my skills but also strengthened my determination to advocate for a more accessible, inclusive, and ethical financial landscape.

With more than fifteen years of experience as a consultant and manager, I have worked with leading multinational corporations such as Renault Sport F1, Air Liquide, L'Oréal, and Lazard Bank, contributing to projects in digital transformation and strategic advisory. These experiences have given me a deep understanding of large-scale financial challenges and allowed me to closely observe the limitations of the conventional system. My certifications in finance and management information systems (SAP Finance & Controlling) have further enabled me to bridge finance and technology—two domains that have become inseparable in today's world.

Through this book, I aim to demonstrate that Islamic finance is far more than a mere alternative: it is a model capable of competing with traditional systems in terms of performance, while simultaneously offering an ethical dimension often absent in conventional finance. This work presents concrete case studies and data-driven analyses, allowing for a rigorous comparison of the two systems. Insights from scholars and experts in the field further enrich this approach, offering diverse and informed perspectives.

My ambition is straightforward: to make Islamic finance both understandable and accessible to all, while contributing to a broader debate on ethics and sustainability in the financial sector. In reading this book, I hope you will discover not only a viable alternative but also a vision for a fairer and more equitable economic future.

# 3. Definition of Islamic Finance

## 3.1 Concept of Islamic Finance

Islamic finance refers to a financial system that complies with the principles of Sharia, or Islamic law. It is not limited to a set of financial products, but rather encompasses a broader framework of ethical and moral rules governing economic transactions. *"And do not consume one another's wealth unjustly, nor offer it [in bribery] to the rulers so that [they might aid] you to consume a portion of the wealth of the people in sin, while you know [it is unlawful].*[1]

The primary objective of Islamic finance is to promote social justice, equity, and economic well-being while avoiding practices deemed illicit (*haram*). Islamic finance thus presents itself as a genuine alternative to conventional finance.[2]

## 3.2 Fundamental Principles

### 3.2.1 Prohibition of Interest (Riba)

**Definition**: *Riba* refers to any gain derived from a loan without a corresponding productive activity. It is strictly prohibited in Islamic finance, as it is considered exploitative. As Visser notes, the prohibition of *riba* is fundamental to Islamic finance since it seeks to foster

---

[1] Qur'an 2 :188.

[2] Hans Visser, *Islamic Finance : Principles and Practice* (2009, page 10).

fairness and equity in transactions, preventing exploitative practices.[3]

**Implication**: Islamic financial institutions cannot lend money in exchange for interest. Instead, they must focus on risk- and profit-sharing arrangements.

### 3.2.2 Profit- and Loss-Sharing

**Concept**: Islamic finance is built on equitable partnerships where both investors and entrepreneurs share risks and profits. This is implemented through contracts such as *Mudarabah* (trust-based partnership) and *Musharakah* (joint venture).

**Impact**: This model encourages all parties to act with greater diligence and responsibility in resource management.

### 3.2.3 Assets-Backed Investments

**Requirement**: Financial transactions must be backed by tangible assets and must not be speculative in nature. This prevents trading practices based on excessively risky instruments.

**Rationale**: This ensures that funds are invested in projects that generate a real impact on the economy and society.

---

[3] Hans Visser, *Islamic Finance : Principles and Practice* (2009, page XIV).

### 3.2.4 Ethics and Social Responsability

**Values**: Islamic Finance promotes ethical business practices aligned with Islamic values. It prohibits investments in sectors such as alcohol, tobacco, gambling, and other activities considered harmful to society.

As an ethical and responsible financial system, it forbids financing activities or products that contradict moral standards. Consequently, investments directly or indirectly linked to addictive products are prohibited under Sharia.[4]

**Objectives**: To foster sustainable and responsible development—economically and socially.

## 3.3 Differences with Conventional Finance

### 3.3.1 Risk Approch

**Islamic finance**: Risk must be shared among the parties involved, thereby encouraging prudent management.

**Conventional finance**: Risk is often transferred entirely to the borrower, potentially leading to situations of excessive indebtedness.

[4] Wadi Mzid, *Islamic Finance: Fundamental Principles and Potential Contributions to Growth and Development Financing*, Economic Agenda of Islamic actors (2011, page 56).

### 3.3.2 Nature of Financial Products

**Islamic finance**: Products must comply with Sharia and be tied to real economic transactions. This excludes certain financial instruments, such as options and futures. In this framework, money is viewed solely as a medium of exchange, not as an asset in itself. Consequently, an Islamic financial contract must involve a real underlying asset.[5]

**Conventional finance**: The range of products is broader and includes derivative instruments that may lack connection to tangible assets.

### 3.3.3 Role of Sharia

**Islamic finance**: Financial decisions are made in accordance with Islamic principles, often under the guidance of a Sharia Supervisory Board. As noted, Islamic finance "is an industry built on prohibition," yet "Muslim jurists and legal theorists have argued that God never forbids anything that is inherently good.".[6]

**Conventional finance**: Decisions are generally guided by profit maximization, with little or no consideration of ethical dimensions.

## 3.4 Importance of Islamique Finance

### 3.4.1 Financial Inclusion

---

[5] François Gueranger, *Islamique Finance : An Illustration of Ethical Finance* (2009, page 72).
[6] Mahmoud El-Gamal, *Islamic Finance* (2006, page 40).

Islamic finance plays a key role in bringing unbanked populations into the financial system by offering products tailored to their needs while respecting their religious beliefs.

### 3.4.2 Economic Development

Islamic finance plays a key role in bringing unbanked populations into the financial system by offering products tailored to their needs while respecting their religious beliefs.

### 3.4.3 Financial Stability

By avoiding excessive indebtedness and focusing on asset-backed investments, Islamic finance can enhance overall financial stability.

### 3.4.4 Social Responsability

Islamic finance emphasizes ethical business practices, which can strengthen corporate reputation and consumer trust. Social responsibility is manifested, among other ways, through the prohibition of *riba*, viewed as a form of social and economic exploitation that contravenes Islam's fundamental teaching on social justice.[7]

**Conclusion:**

Islamic finance represents a unique and ethical approach to financial activity, striving to reconcile economic objectives with moral and social values. It offers

---

[7] Iqbal and Mirakhor, *An Introduction to Islamic Finance* (2011, page 64).

a viable alternative to conventional financial systems, especially in a world increasingly focused on sustainability and social responsibility. By understanding its core principles and implications, economic actors can better navigate this rapidly expanding field.

# 4. Fundamental Principles: Cases Studies, Historical Analyses, and Practical Examples

## 4.1 Case Study: The Mudarabah Contract at Al Rajhi Bank

**Context:** *Mudarabah* is a partnership contract in which one party provides the capital (*rab al-mal*) while the other manages the project (*mudarib*). This model enables entrepreneurs to access financing without resorting to interest.

**Concrete Example:** Real Estate Development Projet

**Situation:** A construction company in Riyadh seeks to develop a residential complex but lacks sufficient equity. It approaches Al Rajhi Bank.

**Process:**

- **Proposal:** The company presents its project to the bank, including market studies and financial forecasts.
- **Agreements:** The bank agrees to finance 70% of the project's cost in exchange for 60% of the profits.
    - **Execution:** Once the complex is completed and sold, profits are shared according to the agreed ratio.

**Outcome:** This model enabled the company to realize its project without bearing a heavy debt burden, while providing the bank with a return on investment tied to performance.

**Lesson Learned:** *Mudarabah* fosters alignment of interests between investor and entrepreneur, thereby reducing the risk of business failure.

## 4.2 Historical Analysis: The Role of Riba in the Economy

**Historical Context:** The prohibition of *riba* (interest) is deeply rooted in Islamic texts and is central to fostering an ethical economy. It refers to charging financial interest or a premium above the principal of a loan.[8]

"Those who consume interest will not stand [on the Day of Resurrection] except as one stands who is being beaten by Satan into insanity. That is because they say, 'Trade is just like interest.' But Allah has permitted trade and forbidden interest."[9]

**Concrete Example: Impact in the Islamic Word**

- **Origins:** In pre-Islamic Arabia, lenders often exploited borrowers through usurious rates, making repayment impossible.

---

[8] Iqbal and Mirakhor, *An Introduction to Islamic Finance* (2011, page 57).
[9] Qur'an 2 : 275.

- **Change:** Following the Qur'anic revelation, the prohibition of *riba* encouraged the rise of economic models based on risk- and profit-sharing, leading to fairer partnerships and greater economic stability.

**Lesson Learned:** The ban on *riba* established an ethical framework for financial transactions centered on social justice and equity.

## 4.3 Practical Examples of Fundamental Principles

### 4.3.1 Mudarabah

**Example:** Al Baraka Bank (Tunisia) uses *Mudarabah* to finance small and medium-sized enterprises (SMEs), providing capital in exchange for a share of profits. One SME in the handicraft sector expanded production through this model, focusing on its core business without bearing interest-based debt.

### 4.3.2 Ijara (Leasing)

**Example:** A transport company in Dubai wishes to acquire trucks. Instead of a conventional loan, it enters into an *Ijara* contract with an Islamic bank. The bank purchases the trucks and leases them to the company for five years. At the end of the period, the company may purchase the trucks at a pre-agreed residual price. This helps manage cash-flow while avoiding interest charges.

### 4.3.3 Musharakah (Partnership)

**Example:** A group of investors pools resources to fund a tech startup under a *Musharakah* agreement. Each contributes capital and shares profits according to a pre-agreed ratio.[10] This model allowed a startup in Indonesia to raise funds while maintaining significant ownership and control.

### 4.3.4 Sukuk (Islamic Bonds)

**Example:** The Malaysian government issues *Sukuk* to finance infrastructure projects such as roads and bridges. Investors purchase *Sukuk* and earn returns based on the revenues generated by the project rather than interest. This mobilizes development funding while complying with Sharia principles.

### 4.3.5 Takaful (Islamic Insurance)

**Example:** Takaful Malaysia offers insurance products based on solidarity. Participants contribute to a common fund used to cover claims. Any surplus is redistributed to participants, unlike conventional insurers where profits go to shareholders.

**Key Note:** Islamic finance rests on risk-sharing in its various forms and generally discourages risk transfer, particularly through debt financing based on interest.[11]

---

[10] Muhammad Taqi Usmani, *An Introduction to Islamic Finance* (2021, page 1).
[11] Iqbal and Mirakhor, *An Introduction to Islamic Finance* (2011, page 109).

## 4.4 Quantitative Case Studies: Example 1 : Real Estate Financing

### 4.4.1 Conventional Financing: Mortgage Loan with Interest

In a conventional financing model, let us consider the example of a borrower who wishes to purchase a house valued at €200,000 through a 20-year mortgage loan at an annual interest rate of 5%%.

- **Property Value :** €200,000
- **Annual Interest Rate :** 5 %
- **Loan Term :** 20 years

The calculation of the monthly installments for this loan is based on the standard amortization formula :

$$M = \frac{P \times r \times (1 + r)^n}{(1 + r)^n - 1}$$

Where :

- M is the monthly installment,
- P is the loan principal (€200 000),
- r is the monthly interest rate (0.05 / 12 = 0.004167)
- n is the total of monthly installments (20 years × 12 = 240).

The calculation results in a monthly installment of approximately **€1,319.91**.

- **Total amount repaid over 20 years:** €1,319.91 × 240 = **€316,778.40**

- **Total interest paid:** €316,778.40 - €200,000 = **116 778,40 €**

### 4.4.2 Islamic Financing: Mourabaha Contract

In Islamic finance, the *Murabaha* contract is commonly used for real estate purchases. Instead of borrowing with interest, the bank buys the house on behalf of the client and then sells it to them at a pre-agreed marked-up price.

- **Bank's purchase price of the house:** €200,000
- **Agreed markup:** 5 % per year over 20 yeras (cumulative)
- **Final price of the client:** €200,000 + total markup = €200,000 × (1 + 0.05 × 20) = €400,000

The client will thus repay €400,000 over 20 years, resulting in monthly payments of €1,666.67

- **Total repaid:** €1,666.67 × 240 = **€400,000**
- **Cost difference compared to the conventional model:** €400,000 – €316,778.40 = **€83,221.60**

**Analysis**

- **Cost:** Though more expensive, *Murabaha* avoids prohibited interest, ensuring ethical compliance.
- **Risk:** In *Murabaha*, the bank initially assumes asset risk, unlike conventional mortgages.
- **Social Responsability:** Islamic finance emphasizes transparency and predictability of payments, whereas conventional loans may expose borrowers to interest rate fluctuations.

## 4.5 Example 2: Business Financing

### 4.5.1 Conventional Financing: Fixed-rate Loan

A company wishes to borrow €1,000,000 to finance an expansion project. The loan is granted over 10 years with a fixed interest rate of 6%.

- **Loan amount :** €1,000,000
- **Annual Interest Rate :** 6 %
- **Term :** 10 years

Using the standard amortization formula, the monthly installment for this loan is approximately €11,102.62.

- **Total repaid over 10 years :** €11,102.62 × 120 = **€1,332 314.40**
- **Total interest paid :** €1,332 314.40 – €1,000,000 = **€332,314.40**

### 4.5.2 Islamic Financing: Moudarabah Contract

In Islamic finance, *Mudarabah* is a partnership in which one party (the *rab al-mal*) provides the capital, while the other (the *mudarib*) manages the project and contributes expertise. Profits are shared according to a pre-agreed ratio, but if the project incurs a loss, it is borne solely by the capital provider.

The concept of profit-sharing is a key element in Islamic finance, reflecting the core values of Islam, namely justice, social equity, and solidarity. The prohibition of interest and the principle of profit-and-loss sharing go hand in hand.

This mechanism serves as an alternative to lender remuneration in the absence of interest. It is defined as a financial system that links capital to industry and commerce without using interest.[12]

- **Amount financed:** €1,000 ,000
- **Agreed profit-sharing:** 60 % for the bank, 40 % for the business
- **Profit generated by the projet:** €500,000 (sur 10 yeras)

In this case, the bank receives €300,000 (60% of €500,000 in profits), while the business retains €200,000.

**Analysis:**

- **Cost:** Under conventional lending, interest is due regardless of project success. In *Mudarabah*, bank returns depend on project performance.
- **Risk-Sharing:** Conventional loans place all risk on the borrower, whereas *Mudarabah* shares risks.
- **Ethics:** Islamic finance emphasizes partnership and fairness, unlike the transaction-driven logic of conventional finance.

**Conclusion: The Superiority of Islamic Finance Through Practical Evidence**

The in-depth analysis of the practical examples and case studies presented in this section underscores the

---

[12] Khan Shahrukh Rafi, *An Economic Analysis of a PLS model for the Financial Sector* », Pakistan Journal of Applied Economics, vol.3, no. 2 (1984, pages 89-105).

relevance of Islamic finance as a model that is not only ethical but also economically viable. Comparative studies between conventional and Islamic financing reveal fundamental differences that position Islamic finance strongly to address current global economic challenges.

Conventional financing models, based on interest (*riba*) and excessive speculation, often generate cycles of debt that burden businesses and households. As several practical examples in this section have shown, these systems can lead to economic imbalances, liquidity crises, and a concentration of wealth at the top of the economic pyramid. In contrast, Islamic finance, by prohibiting interest and promoting equitable practices such as *Mudarabah* (profit- and loss-sharing) and *Musharakah* (partnership), establishes a more balanced relationship among financial actors. This reduces excessive risk, encourages fairer wealth distribution, and supports sustainable growth.

In the comparative examples discussed, the numerical results also show that companies benefiting from Islamic financing, based on risk-sharing, often demonstrate greater long-term resilience. This is reflected in enhanced financial stability, particularly during crises, where the absence of heavy debt allows businesses to better navigate economic turbulence.

A closer examination of the implementation of Islamic contracts, such as *Murabaha* and *Ijara*, reveals that they provide fairer and more transparent financial solutions. These contracts are particularly suitable for small and medium-sized enterprises (SMEs), offering investment opportunities without the cumulative interest constraints characteristic of conventional loans. The quantified examples studied demonstrate that, over the long term, Islamic finance fosters healthier dynamics for job creation and innovation while minimizing the risk of over-indebtedness.

Finally, historical case studies show that Islamic financial systems have withstood periods of global economic crises due to their intrinsically shock-resistant structure. Compared with the cyclical collapses observed in interest-based economies, Islamic systems offer stability that could become a crucial pillar for international financial markets in the future.

**Challenges and Perspectives:** The study of practical examples demonstrates that Islamic finance, far from being merely an alternative model, presents a potential solution to the current weaknesses of global financial systems. By moving away from speculative practices and excessive debt structures, Islamic finance addresses the growing demand for more ethical and sustainable financial solutions.

**The outlook is promising:** as global economies seek ways to support more inclusive and sustainable growth, the principles of Islamic finance—centered on justice, equity, and risk-sharing—are well-positioned to meet these needs. In an increasingly uncertain global context, Islamic finance could become an essential model for long-term economic resilience while promoting fairer and more equitable financial systems for all.

## 4.6 Interview with Dr. Muhammad Imran Ashraf Usmani[13]

Dr. Muhammad Usmani, a prominent scholar of Islamic law and Islamic finance, has made significant contributions to the development of Islamic financial products worldwide. Excerpts are drawn from his publications and presentations.

**1. Why is the prohibition of *riba* so central in Islamic finance?**

*« Riba is forbidden because of its unjust impact on vulnerable segments of society. Sharia seeks to protect fairness and eliminate exploitation. By prohibiting* riba, *Islamic finance ensures that commercial transactions are based on equitable sharing of risks and profits, thereby fostering a fairer and more sustainable economy. »*

**2. How can *Mudarabah* and *Musharakah* transform modern economies?**

*« These contracts encourage shared risk-taking, where both investors and entrepreneurs contribute to the success—or failure—of a project. This differs from debt-based finance where the burden rests solely on the borrower. They provide a platform for entrepreneurial*

[13] Muhammad Imran Ashraf Usmani, Interview conducted on January 25 in Karachi, Pakistan, during the Islamic Finance Conference organized by Dar Al Sharia.

*development and promote an economy grounded in fairness. »*

**3. What challenges exist in applying these principles on a large scale?**

*« One major challenge is harmonizing Sharia interpretations across jurisdictions. Each country may follow a different legal school, making product standardization complex. Moreover, integrating these principles into a global system dominated by conventional finance requires significant efforts in awareness and adaptation. »*

**4. What role do scholars play in the evolution of Islamic financial products?**

*« Scholars play a central role by ensuring compliance with Sharia principles. Their legal expertise is crucial for adapting traditional concepts to modern economic demands, while preserving ethical integrity and Islamic authenticity. »*

# 5. Differences with Conventional Finance: Case Studies & Analyses

## 5.1 Main Differences Between Islamic Finance and Conventional Finance

### 5.1.1 Prohibition of Riba (Interest)

**Islamic finance**: Any form of interest is strictly prohibited. Islamic institutions offer alternatives such as Mudarabah and Musharakah contracts, which are based on risk and profit-sharing.

"O you who believe! Fear Allah and give up what remains of interest, if you are truly believers. And if you do not, then be aware that you are at war with Allah and His Messenger."[14]

**Conventional finance**: Interest is the foundation of lending. Banks lend money with fixed or variable interest rates, which can lead to excessive debt.

### 5.1.2 Risk Sharing

**Islamic finance**: Contracts are designed to share risk between parties. Profits and losses are distributed according to mutual agreements, promoting shared responsibility.

[14] Qur'an 8:27.

**Conventional finance**: Risks are often borne by the borrower, who must repay the principal and interest regardless of investment performance.

### 5.1.3 Ethics and Objectives

**Islamic finance**: Transactions must comply with Shariah, which includes ethical considerations. Investments in haram sectors (e.g., alcohol, tobacco) are prohibited.

**Conventional finance**: Investment decisions are generally based solely on financial returns, without ethical considerations.

In general, four main motives justify entering into a contract: risk-sharing, risk transfer, incentive alignment, or transaction cost minimization. Mudarabah and Musharakah are examples of risk-sharing contracts.[15]

## 5.2 Case Study: Comparison Between an Islamic Bank and a Conventional Bank in Malaysia

**Context**: Malaysia provides a relevant example with both Islamic and conventional banks operating side by side. We will compare Maybank (conventional) and Bank Islam Malaysia Berhad (Islamic).

---

[15] Iqbal and Mirakhor, *Economic Development and Islamic Finance* (2013, page 38).

### 5.2.1 Product : Home Loan

**Maybank (Conventional Bank):**

- **Structure:** Offers home loans with a fixed interest rate of 4% over 20 years.
- **Risk:** The borrower bears all risks. In case of job loss, repayment continues, potentially creating financial hardship.
- **Loan amount:** \$100,000
- **Fixed interest rate:** 4% over 20 years (240 months)
- **Monthly payment:** \$605.98
- **Total repaid after 20 years:** \$605.98 × 240 = \$145,435.20
- **Total interest paid:** \$145,435.20 - \$100,000 = \$45,435.20

In the conventional model, the borrower repays \$145,435.20 over 20 years, with \$45,435.20 as interest. Even if financial circumstances change, the borrower must continue monthly payments. Job loss or financial difficulty increases personal risk.

**Bank Islam Malaysia Berhad (Islamic Bank):**

- **Structure:** Uses a Murabaha contract, where the bank purchases the property and resells it to the borrower at a pre-agreed markup. Repayment is staggered with no interest.
- **Risk:** Risk is shared; the bank remains involved in managing the asset until the borrower fully acquires it.
- **Initial amount:** \$100,000
- **Markup:** 15% (final sale price = \$115,000)

- **Monthly payment:** $479.17
- **Total repaid after 20 years:** $479.17 × 240 = $115,000
- **Additional cost (markup):** $115,000 - $100,000 = $15,000

In the Murabaha model, the bank buys the property for $100,000 and sells it to the borrower for $115,000, with payments spread over 20 years. The total cost is significantly lower than conventional interest.

**Critical Analysis:**

- **Accessibility**: Maybank loans may seem attractive due to speed and familiarity but can trap borrowers in debt cycles. Bank Islam products, though slightly more complex, provide a fairer framework.

- **Resilience**: During the 2008 financial crisis, Islamic banks showed superior resilience as they were not exposed to risky derivatives linked to interest-based lending.

### 5.2.2 Comparative Analysis: Conventional Loan vs Murabaha Financing

**Total amount repaid:**

- **Conventional financing**: $145,435.20 ($45,435.20 in interest)
- **Murabaha financing**: $115,000 ($15,000 markup)

=> **Murabaha** is clearly less costly, with a $30,435.20 advantage for the borrower.

**Risk:**

- **Conventional loan**: Borrower bears all risks, including job loss or income reduction. Default may lead to asset seizure.
- **Murabaha**: Risk is shared; the bank remains engaged until full asset transfer, offering borrower protection.

**Transparency and ethics:**

- **Conventional**: Interest may vary, creating uncertainty; high cost unrelated to investment performance.
- **Murabaha**: No interest; price is fixed and known in advance, complying with Islamic ethical standards.

**Flexibility and adaptability:**

- **Conventional**: Repayment is rigid, even during financial hardship.
- **Murabaha**: More flexible, with risk-sharing and bank involvement during asset acquisition.

**Conclusion:**

Murabaha financing provides significant advantages in cost, risk-sharing, and transparency. Islamic finance promotes ethical, equitable solutions and economic stability, especially during crises, unlike conventional interest-based models.

## 5.3 Concrete Examples of Fundamental Differences

### 5.3.1 Mudarabah Product vs Interest-Based Loan

**Mudarabah Example:** A technology startup receives $500,000 from an Islamic bank through a Mudarabah contract. If the company earns a profit of $200,000, the bank takes 60% and the entrepreneur retains 40%.

- **Financing amount:** $500,000
- **Contract type:** Profit and loss sharing (Mudarabah)
- **Company outcome:** $200,000 profit
- **Profit distribution:**
  - **Bank:** 60% of profits = $120,000
  - **Entrepreneur:** 40% of profits = $80,000

In this scenario, both profit and risk are shared. If the business incurs losses, the entrepreneur is not obliged to repay the initial capital, unlike a conventional loan. This provides flexibility in case of business failure.

**Interest-Based Loan Example:**

Another startup receives a $500,000 loan from a conventional bank at a 5% interest rate. After one year, it must repay $525,000 regardless of success.

- **Financing amount:** $500,000
- **Contract type:** Fixed-rate loan
- **Interest rate:** 5%
- **Repayment after one year:** $525,000

The entrepreneur must repay $525,000 even if losses occur or profits are insufficient. Fixed repayment obligations exist regardless of business performance.

### 5.3.2 Comparative Analysis: Advantages of Islamic Finance vs Conventional Finance

**Risk and profit sharing :**

- **Mudarabah** is a contract based on equitable risk and profit sharing between entrepreneur and investor, encouraging collaboration and avoiding excessive debt during economic difficulty.
- In **conventional finance**, capital and interest repayment is mandatory, creating significant financial stress in case of poor results.

**Absence of riba (interest) in Islamic finance:**

- Islamic finance strictly forbids riba, seen as exploitative.
- **Riba al-nasiah:** Interest on loans in exchange for deferred repayment.
- **Riba al-fadl:** Interest from unequal value exchanges.
- In conventional loans, interest increases repayment obligations regardless of business success, potentially exploiting startups and small businesses.
- Islamic finance returns are based on actual business performance, providing a more ethical approach and avoiding financial exploitation.

### 5.3.3 Financial Stability and Mutual Responsibility

In **Islamic finance**, as in Mudarabah, risk is shared, motivating investors to carefully assess project viability before funding, reducing systemic risk from reckless lending.

**Conventional finance**, with mandatory interest payments, may increase financial pressure during economic downturns or operational difficulties, raising the risk of instability if multiple borrower's default.

**Conclusion – Islamic Finance and Riba:**

**Islamic finance** offers notable advantages in fairness and risk sharing, particularly for startups and entrepreneurs.

**Mudarabah** aligns stakeholder interests and encourages shared responsibility. Unlike conventional finance, it eliminates fixed repayment burdens and interest, which is critical for startups in uncertain economic environments.

Ethical and profit-sharing approaches contribute to a more stable, sustainable financial system, particularly in a world prone to repeated financial crises.

### 5.3.4 Ijara vs Conventional Leasing

**Ijara Example**: A company leases equipment under an Ijara contract, with an option to purchase at the end, reducing total loss risk in case of business failure.

- **Equipment cost:** $100,000
- **Lease duration:** 5 years
- **Monthly Ijara payment:** $1,800
- **Total lease payments over 5 years:** $1,800 × 12 × 5 = $108,000
- **Residual purchase price at contract end:** $20,000

**Scenario – Ijara:**

- Total lease payments: $108,000
- Purchase option exercised: $20,000
- **Total cost if purchased:** $108,000 + $20,000 = $128,000

**Advantage:** If the equipment remains functional and valuable after 5 years, the company can purchase it at a reduced price, protecting the investment and minimizing total loss.

**Conventional Lease Example:**

The same equipment is leased without a purchase option.

- **Monthly payment:** $1,600
- **Total payments over 5 years:** $1,600 × 12 × 5 = $96,000

**Scenario – Conventional Lease:**

- Total payments: $96,000
- No ownership at the end of lease
- **Outcome:** Equipment is returned to the owner; if it becomes obsolete, the company loses the full capital invested.

## Comparison of Results:

The following comparison highlights the key differences between an **Ijara contract** and a **conventional lease**. While both provide access to assets through periodic payments, their **cost structures, ownership options, risk allocation, and flexibility** diverge significantly. This analysis illustrates how Ijara offers not only financial utility but also ethical and strategic advantages aligned with Shariah principles.

| Feature | Ijara | Conventional Lease |
|---|---|---|
| Total cost over 5 years | $108,000 + $20,000 = $128,000 | $96,000 |
| Ownership at end | Option to purchase for $20,000 | None |
| Investment risk | Reduced, can retain value if purchased | Full, no return if obsolete |
| Flexibility | High, purchase option available | Low, no option |

*Table 5.1: Comparison Ijara vs Conventional Lease.*

## Enhanced Conclusion & Lessons:

- Although Ijara has a higher nominal cost ($128,000 vs $96,000), it provides **flexibility and risk mitigation**, particularly in volatile markets or for assets with potential rapid obsolescence.
- If the equipment retains value or can be resold, Ijara may be **more economically advantageous long-term**.
- Conventional leasing avoids additional payments but leaves the company with **no ownership or return on investment**, increasing vulnerability to asset depreciation.
- **Lesson:** Islamic finance instruments like Ijara prioritize **shared responsibility, risk management, and long-term strategic value** over short-term savings, making them suitable for uncertain or high-risk environments.

### 5.3.5 Sukuk vs Conventional Bonds

**Sukuk Example:** A government issues $100 million Sukuk to finance an infrastructure project. Investors receive payments based on the revenue generated by the project.

- **Issue amount:** $100 million
- **Revenue-based structure:** e.g., toll bridge
- **Duration:** 5 years
- **Annual revenue generated:** $20 million
- **Revenue share for investors:** 75%

**Calculations:**

- Annual distribution : 75% × $20 million = $15 million
- Total received over 5 years: $15 million × 5 = $75 million

Investors are paid only from project revenues; payments vary with performance.

**Conventional Bond Example:**

A company issues $100 million bonds with 5% fixed interest.

- Annual interest: 5% × $100 million = $5 million
- Total interest over 5 years: $5 million × 5 = $25 million
- Capital repayment at maturity: $100 million
- **Total received by investors:** $25 million + $100 million = $125 million

## Comparison of Results:

The following comparison examines the fundamental distinctions between **Sukuk** and **conventional bonds**. Although both instruments serve as vehicles for raising capital, they differ significantly in their **structure, risk allocation, investor returns, and compliance frameworks**. Sukuk emphasize asset-backed financing and shared risk in line with Shariah principles, while conventional bonds operate on fixed interest payments and guaranteed capital repayment.

| Feature | Sukuk | Conventional Bond |
|---|---|---|
| Total received by investors | $75 million | $125 million |
| Capital repayment | No | Yes ($100 million) |
| Payment variability | Yes, depends on project revenue | No, fixed |
| Risk exposure | Shared with project performance | Investor protected |
| Ethical compliance | Sharia-compliant, no interest | Conventional interest |

*Table 5.2: Comparison Sukuk vs Conventional Bonds.*

## Enhanced Conclusion & Lessons :

- Conventional bonds deliver **fixed returns and capital protection**, making them attractive for risk-averse investors.
- Sukuk ties investor returns to **real asset performance**, aligning incentives between issuer and investor and **sharing both profits and losses**.
- Sukuk promotes **ethical and sustainable finance**, avoiding riba (interest) and investing in tangible assets.
- While nominal returns on Sukuk may appear lower, they **reflect actual economic value** and encourage careful project assessment and financial discipline.
- **Lesson:** Sukuk demonstrates how Islamic finance can **align investor interests with real economic**

**activity**, reduce speculative risk, and foster ethical investment frameworks

## 5.4 Interview with an Islamic Finance Expert: Dr. Aisha Yousuf[16]

Dr. Aisha Yousuf is a respected Islamic finance scholar and a member of the Shariah Advisory Council at the International Islamic Liquidity Management Corporation (IILM). Excerpts from an interview based on her teachings and publications.

**1. Key advantages of Islamic finance over conventional finance?**

*« Islamic finance is based on equity, justice, and risk-sharing. Unlike conventional finance, focused on profit maximization via interest rates, Islamic finance aims to balance financial returns with social responsibility. It also provides an ethical framework, prohibiting investments in harmful sectors such as alcohol, gambling, and weapons, making it more sustainable and aligned with social justice values. »*

**2. How can Islamic finance meet the needs of modern businesses?**

*« Islamic finance offers flexible solutions like Mudarabah and Musharakah contracts, enabling companies to access funding without excessive debt. Modern businesses, especially in emerging markets, seek*

[16] Aisha Yousuf, interview conducted on April 22, 2019, in Kuala Lumpur, Malaysia, during the International Islamic Finance Congress.

*alternatives that allow growth while minimizing financial risks. By relying on profit-and-loss sharing instead of interest, Islamic finance provides an equitable solution. »*

**3. What are the main criticisms of Islamic finance, and how can they be addressed?**

*« A common critique is the complexity of Islamic financial products, particularly regarding Shariah compliance. The solution lies in market education. We need to raise awareness among investors, regulators, and businesses about the benefits of Islamic models. Additionally, greater harmonization of international standards would reduce confusion and improve transparency. »*

**4. How do you see the future of Islamic finance in the global financial landscape?**

*« Islamic finance has a key role to play in the future global economy, especially with the rise of sustainable and ethical finance practices. With the growth of ESG (Environmental, Social, Governance) investments, the principles of Islamic finance perfectly align with sustainability goals. Its integration into the global financial system will only increase, with more countries and institutions adopting Shariah-compliant products. »*

# 6. Concrete Examples of Islamic Financing: Detailed Case Studies

## 6.1 Case Study: Real Estate Project Financing via Mudarabah

**Context:** Mudarabah is a partnership contract that allows an investor to finance a project managed by an entrepreneur. This case focuses on a real estate project in Saudi Arabia.

**Project:** Residential complex development in Jeddah

### 6.1.1 Mudarabah Financing

- **Investor:** Al Baraka Bank
- **Entrepreneur :** Local construction company

**Process :**

1. **Project Proposal:** The construction company presents a detailed plan, including a market study, projected budget, and implementation schedule.
2. **Financing Agreement:** The bank agrees to finance **70% of the costs (10,000,000 SAR)** in exchange for **60% of net profits**.
3. **Execution:** The project is completed, and the units are sold.

**Results and Calculations:**

- **Total project cost:** 14,285,714 SAR (bank finances 10,000,000 SAR = 70% of total).
- **Net profit after 1 year:** 3,000,000 SAR

**Profit sharing :**

- Bank (60%) : 3,000,000 × 0.6 = **1,800,000 SAR**
- Entrepreneur (40%) : 3,000,000 × 0.4 = **1,200,000 SAR**

**Analysis:**

- The entrepreneur benefits from significant capital without interest obligations.
- Shared profit incentives encourage efficient project management.
- Risk is partly transferred to the bank, aligning both parties' interests.

### 6.1.2 Conventional Loan Analysis (Interest-based Financing)

**Project Proposition**: The construction company requests a conventional bank loan of **10 million SAR** to finance **70% of the project**, at an annual interest rate of **5%**.

**Financing Agreement:**

The company is required to repay the full principal amount plus interest, regardless of the project's profitability.

**Calculations:**

- **Loan principal :** 10,000,000 SAR
- **Annual interest:** 10,000,000 × 0.05 = **500,000 SAR**

- **Total repayment after 1 year:** 10,000,000 + 500,000 = **10,500,000 SAR**

**Net profit after repayment:**

- Net project profit : 3,000,000 SAR
- Less interest : 3,000,000 - 500,000 = **2,500,000 SAR**

**Comparison:**

- Bank's interest is fixed, regardless of project performance.
- Entrepreneur bears full financial risk if the project underperforms.

**Implication :**

- The bank receives a fixed return (500,000 SAR interest) irrespective of the project outcome.
- The company bears all operational and financial risk, as repayment obligations remain constant even if the project underperforms.

### 6.1.3 Comparative Results

The following comparison highlights the key differences between a **Mudarabah contract** and a **conventional loan**. While both provide financing to entrepreneurs, their structures diverge in terms of **profit distribution, risk allocation, and payment flexibility**. Mudarabah emphasizes shared risk and proportional returns, whereas conventional loans impose fixed repayments regardless of project performance:

| Metric | Mudarabah (Islamic) | Conventional Loan |
|---|---|---|
| Entrepreneur net profit | 1,200,000 SAR | 2,500,000 SAR |
| Bank share/profit | 1,800,000 SAR | 500,000 SAR |
| Risk distribution | Shared | Bank insulated, entrepreneur bears all risk |
| Flexibility | Payments proportional to profit | Fixed repayment |

*Table 6.1: Comparison Mudarabah (Islamic) vs Conventional Loan.*

**Conclusion and Lessons :**

- **Islamic financing via Mudarabah** distributes risks and rewards equitably, encouraging sustainable growth.
- **Conventional financing** guarantees bank return but imposes rigid financial obligations on entrepreneurs.
- **Lesson**: Mudarabah promotes alignment between investor and entrepreneur, incentivizing efficiency and reducing default risk.

## 6.2 Case Study: SME Financing via Musharakah

**Context:** Musharakah is a partnership where parties contribute capital and share profits and losses.

**Project:** Launch of a technology startup in Malaysia

**Partners:** Group of investors + tech startup

### 6.2.1 Musharakah Financing (islamic)

- **Capital structure:** Each partner contributes 1,000,000 MYR → Total capital = 2,000,000 MYR
- **Profit sharing:** Startup 70% (manager), Investors 30%

- **Management:** Startup handles operations; investors receive regular reports

**Results:**

- Total profit after 2 years: 500,000 MYR

**Profit distribution :**

  - Startup : 500,000 × 0.7 = **350,000 MYR**
  - Investors : 500,000 × 0.3 = **150,000 MYR**

**Analysis:**

- Startup retains control while accessing capital.
- Risks are shared; losses are proportional.
- Investors gain visibility and potential advisory benefits.

### 6.2.2 Conventionnel Loan Analysis (Bank Interest)

- **Loan amount :** 1,000,000 MYR
- **Interest rate :** 5% per year

**Calculations :**

- Annual interest: 1,000,000 × 0.05 = 50,000 MYR
- Total interest over 2 years: 50,000 × 2 = 100,000 MYR
- Total repayment: 1,000,000 + 100,000 = **1,100,000 MYR**

**Analysis :**

- Startup must repay the full amount plus interest, regardless of profitability.
- Financial pressure is high if profits are low or negative.

### 6.2.3 Comparative Analysis

The comparison below contrasts a **Musharakah partnership** with a **conventional loan**, focusing on profitability, risk-sharing, and financing structure. While Musharakah fosters equitable distribution of both profits and risks between the entrepreneur and investors, conventional loans rely on fixed interest payments, transferring the full burden of risk to the entrepreneur.

| Metric | Musharakah (Islamic) | Conventional Loan |
|---|---|---|
| Entrepreneur net profit | 350,000 MYR | 400,000 MYR |
| Investors / Bank profit | 150,000 MYR | 100,000 MYR |
| Risk distribution | Shared | Entrepreneur bears full risk |
| Interest | None | Fixed 5% |

*Table 6.2: Comparative Analysis.*

**Conclusion and Lessons:**

- Musharakah creates a fairer structure, especially for high-uncertainty growth phases.
- Encourages sustainable growth, reduces financial stress on entrepreneurs, and fosters long-term partnerships.
- Lesson: Risk-sharing financing aligns incentives and protects SMEs from excessive leverage.

## 6.3 Case Study: Equipment Financing via Ijara

**Context:** Ijara is a leasing contract where the asset is rented to the user with an option to purchase at the end.

**Project:** Acquisition of construction cranes for ABC Construction, Egypt.

### 6.3.1 Ijara Financing

- **Cost of equipment:** 1,500,000 LE
- **Monthly lease payment:** 30,000 LE
- **Lease term:** 5 years → 5 × 12 = 60 months

**Calculations:**

- Total lease payments: 30,000 × 60 = **1,800,000 LE**
- Residual purchase price: 200,000 LE
- Total cost if purchased: 1,800,000 + 200,000 = **2,000,000 LE**

### 6.3.2 Conventional Loan Analysis

- **Loan amount :** 1,500,000 LE
- **Interest rate:** 7% per year → 0.583% per month
- **Loan term :** 60 months

**Monthly payment formula :**

$$M = \frac{P \times r \times (1 + r)^n}{(1 + r)^n - 1}$$

**Calculations:**

- Monthly payment ≈ 29,703 LE
- Total repayment : 29,703 × 60 = **1,782,180 LE**
- Total interest : 1,782,180 – 1,500,000 = **282,180 LE**

### 6.3.3 Comparison Analysis

The following comparison highlights the key distinctions between **Ijara financing** and a **conventional loan**, focusing on total costs, ownership outcomes, risk allocation, and contractual flexibility. While Ijara emphasizes shared responsibility and eventual asset ownership, conventional loans provide lower upfront payments but place the full burden of risk on the borrower.

| Metric | Ijara (Islamic) | Conventional Loan |
|---|---|---|
| Total payments | 2,000,000 LE | 1,782,180 LE |
| Ownership at end | Yes (after purchase) | No (unless separately arranged) |
| Risk distribution | Shared with bank | Fully on ABC Construction |
| Flexibility | High | Low |

*Table 6.3: Comparative Analysis.*

**Conclusion and Lessons :**

- **Ijara** allows businesses to access equipment without upfront capital and share risks with the bank.
- **Conventional loans** impose fixed interest and repayment obligations, adding financial pressure.
- **Lesson**: Ijara enhances operational flexibility and risk mitigation, particularly in uncertain or capital-intensive projects.

## 6.4 Case Study: Sukuk Issuance for Infrastructure Financing

**Context:** Sukuk are Islamic financial certificates representing ownership of tangible assets, generating returns without interest.

**Project:** Highway construction in Indonesia

- **Issuer :** Indonesian government
- **Amount raised :** 500 millions USD
- **Term:** 10 years
- **Assumed yield:** 5% per year based on highway revenue

**Calculations:**

- Annual payment to Sukuk holders: 500,000,000 × 0.05 = **25,000,000 USD**
- Total payment over 10 years: 25,000,000 × 10 = **250,000,000 USD**

**Revenue assumption**: Highway generates 50,000,000 USD annually → Sukuk payments are 50% of revenue.

### 6.4.1 Conventional Bond Comparison

- **Interest rate :** 5% fixed
- Annual interest payment: 500,000,000 × 0.05 = 25,000,000 USD
- Total over 10 years: 25,000,000 × 10 = 250,000,000 USD

**Analysis:**

- Fixed interest obliges payment regardless of revenue performance.
- Sukuk payments vary with asset performance, sharing risk with investors.

### 6.4.2 Comparative Analysis

The comparison below outlines the structural and functional differences between **Sukuk** and **conventional bonds**, emphasizing how obligations, risk distribution, and ownership are managed. Sukuk instruments link returns to the performance of underlying assets, offering shared risk and partial ownership, while conventional bonds operate on fixed obligations, insulating investors but placing full liability on the issuer.

| Metric | Sukuk (Islamic) | Conventional Bond |
|---|---|---|
| Payment obligation | Performance-based | Fixed |
| Risk distribution | Shared with investors | Government bears full risk |
| Investor ownership | Partial ownership of asset | Debt holder only |
| Flexibility and sustainability | High | Lower |

*Table 6.4: Comparative Analysis, Sukuk (Islamic) vs Conventional Bond.*

**Conclusion and Lessons:**

- **Sukuk** aligns investors with project performance, reducing financial strain on issuers.
- Encourages ethical, asset-backed investment while enabling infrastructure development.
- **Lesson**: Sukuk integrates risk-sharing and ownership principles, fostering sustainable public financing.

## 6.5 Interview with Dr. Abbas Mirakhor[17]

Dr. Abbas Mirakhor is a globally recognized expert in Islamic finance and a former Executive Director at the International Monetary Fund (IMF). The following are excerpts from interviews and writings on the role of Islamic contracts in supporting entrepreneurs and the challenges faced by Islamic financial institutions.

**1. How do you assess the role of Mudarabah and Musharakah contracts in supporting entrepreneurs?**

« *Mudarabah and Musharakah contracts provide a unique framework for supporting entrepreneurs by sharing both risks and rewards. Unlike conventional financing systems, where investors demand a fixed return, these models encourage innovation and risk-taking. They also create synergy among stakeholders, who become partners in the success of the enterprise.* This fosters long-term investment and alignment of interests. »

**2. What lessons can be drawn from the case studies you have observed?**

« *One of the key lessons from Islamic finance case studies is that these models can genuinely stimulate inclusive economic development. The examples demonstrate that Islamic finance, by emphasizing risk-sharing and partnerships, can help small and medium-sized enterprises (SMEs) grow without the risks associated with excessive debt. These studies also illustrate how the*

[17] Abbas Mirakhor, Interview réalisé le 10 juin à Washington, D.C., États-Unis, lors d'un symposium organisé par l'Islamic Development Bank (IDB).

*ethical principles of Islamic finance contribute to sustainable and socially responsible development. »*

**3. What challenges do Islamic financial institutions face in implementing these models?**

*« The main challenge facing Islamic financial institutions is education and awareness. Many people, including entrepreneurs and investors, do not yet fully understand the advantages of profit-and-loss sharing financing systems. Furthermore, it is necessary to establish a robust regulatory infrastructure to support Islamic finance, particularly regarding the standardization and harmonization of rules across different jurisdictions. »*

**4. How do you envision the future of Islamic finance in the global economic context?**

*« With the rise of ethical finance and socially responsible investment (SRI), Islamic finance is well-positioned to play an even more significant role on the global stage. Investors are increasingly seeking options that meet ethical and sustainable criteria, making Islamic finance an attractive choice. I firmly believe that the Islamic principles of justice, risk-sharing, and social responsibility will become standards in the near future.*

# 7. Practical Use and Expansion: Case Studies by Region

## 7.1 Introduction to Islamic Finance in Sub-Saharan Africa

Sub-Saharan Africa, with its economic and cultural diversity, presents significant potential for Islamic finance. This section explores case studies of successful projects, highlighting financing methods and socio-economic impacts.

## 7.2 Case Study: Agricultural Financing in Cameroon Using Mudarabah

**Context:** Cameroon, a country with a strong agricultural sector, requires financing to modernize its agricultural practices. A pilot project was launched with an Islamic bank to support local farmers.

**Project:** Modernization of farms in western Cameroon

**Partners:** Islamic Bank of Cameroon and local agricultural cooperatives

### 7.2.1 Calculation using Mudarabah

**Process :**

- **Needs assessment:** The bank collaborates with cooperatives to identify financing needs for seeds, equipment, and training.
- **Mudarabah agreement:** The bank finances 75% of total costs (approximately 1 million

FCFA) in exchange for 50% of net profits realized by the cooperatives.

- **Implementation:** Farmers use the financing to acquire modern equipment and improve yields.

**Example Data :**

- Total modernization cost: 1,330,000 FCFA
- Bank financing (75%) : 1,000,000 FCFA
- Cooperative financing (25%) : 330,000 FCFA
- Profit-sharing: 50% to the bank, 50% to the cooperatives
- Net profit after modernization : 500,000 FCFA
- Increase in agricultural production : +30%

**Profit-sharing calculations:**

- **Net profit :** 500,000 FCFA
- **Bank share (50%) :** 500,000 × 0.5 = 250,000 FCFA
- **Cooperative share (50%) :** 500,000 × 0.5 = 250,000 FCFA

**Return on Investment (ROI):**

- **Bank :**
  - Initial investment: 1,000,000 FCFA
  - Profit earned : 250,000 FCFA
  - ROI : 250,000 ÷ 1,000,000 × 100 = 25%
- **Cooperatives:**
  - Initial investment : 330,000 FCFA
  - Profit earned : 250,000 FCFA
  - ROI : 250,000 ÷ 330,000 × 100 ≈ 75.76%

**Results :**

- **Production increase:** Cooperatives experienced a 30% increase in agricultural output.
- **Shared profits:** Out of a net profit of 500,000 FCFA, the bank received 250,000 FCFA, promoting partnership sustainability.

**Analysis :**

- **Social impact:** The model improved food security and farmers' income.
- **Risks and challenges:** Climatic variations could affect production, but profit-sharing encouraged proactive management.

### 7.2.2 Comparison with Conventional Financing (Interest-Based Loan)

If the cooperatives had opted for a conventional interest-based loan at 10% per year:

- Loan amount: 1,000,000 FCFA
- Annual interest: 1,000,000 × 0.10 = 100,000 FCFA
- Total repayment after 1 year: 1,000,000 + 100,000 = 1,100,000 FCFA

**Impact on profits :**

- Cooperatives would retain the full net profit of 500,000 FCFA but must repay 1,100,000

FCFA, resulting in a deficit of 600,000 FCFA (1,100,000 – 500,000).

- This model imposes a much higher total cost due to interest, leaving cooperatives with debt despite increased production.

**Conclusion :**

**With Mudarabah:**

- Risk is shared between the bank and cooperatives, and both parties' benefit from project success.
- Cooperatives enhance productivity with modern equipment while sharing profits fairly.
- Bank ROI is reasonable (25%), while cooperatives enjoy a high ROI (75.76%).

**With interest-based loan :**

- Cooperatives bear all financial risk. Even with success, they must repay the loan with interest, reducing actual profit.
- This model imposes additional financial pressure, particularly if production underperforms.

**Lesson:** Islamic finance, particularly Mudarabah, demonstrates its advantage by fostering partnership relations and risk-sharing, encouraging sustainable development, in contrast to conventional loans which impose heavier financial burdens in cases of moderate success.

## 7.3 Case Study: Infrastructure Development Through Sukuk in East Africa

**Context:** East Africa has witnessed a rise in Sukuk issuances to finance essential infrastructure.

**Project:** Construction of a highway in Tanzania

**Issuer:** Tanzanian Government

### 7.3.1 Calculation Using Sukuk

**Process :**

- **Sukuk issuance:** Government issues Sukuk worth \$200 million to fund highway construction.
- **Investors:** Sukuk sold to private and institutional investors, guaranteeing payments based on toll revenues.
- **Use of funds:** Allocated to highway construction and maintenance.

**Example Data :**

- Amount raised: \$200 million
- Annual toll revenues : \$40 millions
- Annual Sukuk yield: 5% of highway revenue
- Term: 10 years

**Calculations :**

- Annual payout to investors : 200,000,000 × 0.05 = 10,000,000 \$

- Total payments over 10 years : 10,000,000 × 10 = 100,000,000 $

**Results :**

- **Rapid fundraising:** Government raised funds efficiently without relying on conventional loans.
- **Investor returns:** Investors receive revenue-based payouts aligned with Islamic finance principles.

**Analysis :**

- **Advantages:** Supports essential infrastructure while complying with Islamic finance.
- **Risks:** Dependence on toll revenues is influenced by traffic fluctuations.

### 7.3.2 Comparison with Conventional Bond Financing

If the Tanzanian government had issued conventional bonds at 5% interest:

- Amount raised: $200 million
- Annual interest payments: 200,000,000 × 0.05 = 10,000,000 $
- Total payments over 10 years: 10,000,000 × 10 = 100,000,000 $

**Differences:**

- Payments are identical in amount but fixed, independent of highway revenue.

- Bondholders receive guaranteed interest regardless of performance.

**Analysis & Conclusion :**

**Sukuk :**

- Returns are linked to asset performance, creating a direct correlation between project success and investor yields.
- Risk is shared; if revenues fall, investors earn less.
- Complies with Islamic principles: no fixed interest (Riba), revenue is asset-based.

**Conventional bonds :**

- Investors receive fixed interest regardless of performance.
- Government bears full financial risk if toll revenues underperform.

**Conclusion:**

Sukuk financing is advantageous for the Tanzanian government as it shares risk with investors while adhering to Islamic principles. Investors earn only if infrastructure generates revenue, motivating project success. Conventional bonds place greater financial risk on the government. Sukuk is more sustainable for long-term infrastructure projects with variable revenue streams.

## 7.4 Case Study: Expansion of Islamic Microfinance in Sub-Saharan Africa

**Context:** Islamic microfinance is emerging as a solution for low-income populations to access funding.

**Project :** Islamic microfinance in Senegal

**Institution :** Takaful Microfinance

**Process :**

- **Takaful model:** Provides interest-free loans using a communal fund contributed by members.
- **Funded projects:** Small-scale enterprises, such as artisan product sales.
- **Support & training:** Takaful provides business management training and fund usage guidance.

**Results :**

- **Economic impact:** Hundreds of women launched businesses, improving financial conditions.
- **Social stability:** Model strengthens member solidarity and support networks.

**Analysis :**

- **Advantages:** Promotes financial inclusion, allowing marginalized groups access to funds without interest.

- **Challenges:** Financial education is crucial for project success.

**Additional challenges :**

- **Complex regulation:** Legal frameworks for Takaful products vary by country, complicating compliance.
- **Limited investment options:** Sharia-compliant investments may restrict portfolio diversification.
- **Competition with conventional insurance:** Takaful competes with established insurers, potentially slowing adoption.
- **Higher administrative costs:** Takaful operational structures may lead to higher costs, impacting competitiveness.

**Note:** The Global Islamic Finance Report (2022) shows that Islamic investments in Sub-Saharan Africa grew by 25% due to rising demand for ethical financing solutions.[18]

---

[18] Global Islamic Finance Report (GIFR).

## 7.5 Interview avec Dr. Mohammad Usman[19]

Dr. Mohammad Usman is a recognized researcher and professor of Islamic finance at the University of Kuala Lumpur and consultant for multiple Islamic financial institutions in Sub-Saharan Africa.

**1. What are the main applications of Islamic finance in Sub-Saharan Africa?**

*« In Sub-Saharan Africa, Islamic finance is primarily applied in agriculture, real estate, and microfinance. Models such as Mudarabah and Musharakah are used to support farmers by providing interest-free funding, which is especially relevant in economies with limited access to credit. This not only enhances agricultural productivity but also contributes to community development. »*

**2. How do you assess the success of Islamic finance projects in Africa?**

*« Case studies show that Islamic finance projects in Africa have achieved notable success, particularly due to their alignment with local cultural and religious values. For example, Islamic microfinance initiatives have enabled many entrepreneurs to start and expand businesses. This demonstrates that Islamic finance is not only about religious compliance but can also deliver tangible economic benefits. »*

---

[19] Mohammad Usman, Interview conducted on August 18, 2017, in Lagos, Nigeria, during the African Islamic Finance Forum.

**3. What specific challenges does Islamic finance face in Sub-Saharan Africa?**

*« One major challenge is the lack of awareness and understanding of Islamic financial products among the population. Regulatory obstacles and standardization issues also complicate the integration of Islamic finance into conventional systems. Additionally, limited financial infrastructure can hinder large-scale project implementation. »*

**4. How do you envision the future of Islamic finance in Sub-Saharan Africa?**

*« The future is promising. With a young and increasingly financially aware population, there is substantial potential for the growth of Islamic financial products. Moreover, increasing partnerships between Islamic banks and microfinance institutions offer opportunities to expand access to funding. I am confident that Islamic finance can play a crucial role in the region's economic development. »*

# 8. Challenges and Opportunities: Current and Future Perspectives

## 8.1 Introduction to the Challenges and Opportunities of Islamic Finance

Islamic finance, which is rapidly expanding, faces specific challenges that can hinder its development. However, it also offers unique opportunities for emerging markets and developing economies. This section explores these challenges and opportunities while examining the future prospects of Islamic finance.

## 8.2 Challenges in Islamic Finance

### 8.2.1 Understanding and Awareness

**Problem:** A large part of the population remains poorly informed about the principles and products of Islamic finance.

**Impact**: This limits the adoption of Islamic financial products and slows their integration into the traditional financial system.

### 8.2.2 Regulation and Legal Framework

**Problem**: Regulatory systems in many countries are not yet adapted to the specificities of Islamic finance.

**Impact**: The absence of clear regulations can lead to legal uncertainties for investors and institutions.

### 8.2.3 Competition with Conventional Finance

**Problem**: Conventional financial institutions still dominate the market.

**Impact:** Competition based on interest rates and attractive products can discourage clients from turning to Islamic finance.

### 8.2.4 Professional Training

**Problem**: here is a shortage of specialists trained in Islamic finance, which limits the available expertise.

**Impact**: This affects service quality, sector innovation, and regulation. The complexity of regulatory challenges in Islamic finance highlights the need to harmonize standards to support growth.[20]

## 8.3 Opportunities in Islamic Finance

### 8.3.1 Global Market Growth

**Situation:** Islamic finance is growing rapidly, with increasing demand for Sharia-compliant products, particularly in Muslim-majority countries.

**Potential:** Islamic financial institutions can capitalize on this trend by expanding their product offerings and targeting new market segments.

---

[20] Muhammad Taqi Usmani, *Islamic Finance: Principles and Practice* (2011, page 45).

### 8.3.2 Green Economy and Sustainable Development

**Situation**: The growing interest in responsible and sustainable investments aligns well with Islamic finance principles.

**Potential**: Islamic financial products can play a key role in financing renewable energy projects and sustainable infrastructure.

### 8.3.3 Financial Inclusion

**Situation**: Islamic finance offers solutions adapted to unbanked or underbanked populations.

**Potential**: By developing microfinance products and targeting disadvantaged segments, Islamic institutions can contribute to financial inclusion.

### 8.3.4 Financial Technology (Fintech)

**Situation**: The rise of fintech offers new avenues for Islamic finance, enabling more accessible and efficient services.

**Potential**: Fintech startups can develop innovative Sharia-compliant solutions, attracting a younger, tech-savvy clientele.

## 8.4 Case Study: Innovations in Islamic Finance and the Impact of Fintech

**Context**: A notable example of innovation in Islamic finance is Wahed Invest, a startup offering halal investment solutions via a digital platform.

### 8.4.1 Offered Product

**Investment Platform**: Wahed Invest allows users to diversify their investment portfolios with Sharia-compliant assets, such as equities and real estate.

**Accessibility**: Users can start investing with small amounts, making Islamic investment accessible to a wider audience.

### 8.4.2 Impact

**Financial Education:** Wahed Invest also provides educational resources to raise awareness of Islamic finance principles.

**Expansion**: Thanks to its digital model, the startup has reached clients in multiple countries, promoting Islamic finance beyond borders.

## 8.5 Prospects for Islamic Finance

### 8.5.1 Evolution of Products

**Trends**: A further diversification of Islamic financial products is expected, including online investment options, halal insurance, and green Sukuk.

**Innovation:** Innovation will continue to be a key driver to attract new clients and meet their needs.

### 8.5.2 Collaboration with conventional Institutions

**Opportunity:** Cooperation between Islamic and conventional institutions can strengthen the credibility of Islamic finance and expand its market.

**Synergies:** This may also lead to the creation of hybrid products combining best practices from both systems.

### 8.5.3 Tailored Regulation

**Necessity**: Efforts must be made to establish clear and suitable regulatory frameworks for Islamic finance.

**Potentiel Impact:** Well-designed regulation could strengthen investor and consumer confidence in Islamic products.

### 8.5.4 Awareness and Education

**Required Actions:** Awareness and educational initiatives will play a crucial role in informing the public and professionals about the advantages and principles of Islamic finance.

**Goal**: This could encourage broader adoption and better understanding of Islamic financial products.

## 8.6 Interview with Dr. Mohamad A. El-Gamal[21]

Dr. Mohamad A. El-Gamal is a renowned economist and professor at Rice University, an expert in Islamic finance, and author of several works on the subject.

**1. What major challenges do you see for Islamic finance in the coming years?**

*« Challenges related to regulation, standards harmonization, and public understanding remain crucial. However, I am convinced that Islamic finance can overcome these obstacles through increased efforts in education and innovation. Awareness of Islamic finance principles and training professionals in the sector are essential to improving perception and adoption of these products. »*

**2. How does technology influence the development of Islamic finance?**

*« Technology, especially fintech, plays a transformative role in the development of Islamic finance. Fintech solutions make Islamic financial services more accessible while facilitating the introduction of innovative and sustainable business models. Crowdfunding platforms and Sharia-compliant investment management apps are becoming increasingly common, opening new avenues for entrepreneurs and investors. »*

---

[21] Mohamad A. El-Gamal, Interview conducted on September 29, 2021, in Houston, Texas, United States, following a lecture at Rice University on Islamic economics.

**3. What opportunities does Islamic finance offer for emerging economies?**

*« Islamic finance has significant potential to stimulate economic development in emerging economies, particularly by providing funds to small and medium-sized enterprises (SMEs) and enhancing financial inclusion. This is especially relevant in regions such as Africa and Asia, where many people lack access to traditional financial services. By integrating ethical and sustainability principles, Islamic finance can meet financial needs while respecting societal values. »*

**4. How do you see the future of Islamic finance globally??**

*« With continuous growth and increasing adoption, I believe Islamic finance will play a major role on the global financial stage, particularly in green economy sectors and responsible investments. The trend towards more sustainable and socially responsible investment practices creates synergies with Islamic finance principles, which could strengthen its position in the global financial landscape. »*

# 9. Evolution of Islamic Fintech

## 9.1 Context and Definition of Islamic Fintech

Islamic fintech combines the principles of Islamic finance with technological innovations to provide Sharia-compliant financial services. Its main goal is to improve access to financial services, particularly for unbanked or underbanked populations.

## 9.2 History of the Emergence of Islamic Fintech

### 9.2.1 Origins in the 2010s

The rise of digital technologies coincided with growing demand for Sharia-compliant financial services, particularly in regions such as Southeast Asia.

### 9.2.2 Examples of Pioneer Platforms

**Wahed Invest (2015)**: Launched to provide halal investment opportunities for a young clientele. By 2021, it had attracted over 250,000 users and managed more than $100 million in assets.

### 9.2.3 Growth in Investments

According to a Statista report, investments in Islamic fintech were estimated at approximately $44 billion in 2022 and are projected to reach $60 billion by 2025.

## 9.3 Key Features of Islamic Fintech

### 9.3.1 Sharia Compliance

Products must be evaluated by a Sharia board, which strengthens user trust.

### 9.3.2 Accessibility and Inclusivity

For example, **Namal Pay** enabled over 50,000 users in rural areas, where banking services are limited, to access Sharia-compliant payment services.

## 9.4 Concrete Examples of Islamic Fintech

### 9.4.1 Wahed Invest

**Features:** By 2021, the platform allowed users to invest in over 100 publicly listed Sharia-compliant companies, diversifying their portfolios.

**Impact:** With average annual returns of 8%, Wahed demonstrated the viability of a halal investment model.

### 9.4.2 Ethis

**Crowdfunding:** Ethis raised over $20 million for projects in Southeast Asia and Africa, funding initiatives such as hospital construction and affordable housing.

**Social Impact:** In 2022, Ethis helped create over 1,000 jobs through its funded projects.

### 9.4.3 Namal Pay

**Growth:** The platform recorded a 150% increase in users in 2023, reaching a total of 100,000 users across the Middle East.

**Impact:** Namal Pay facilitated over $10 million in transactions in 2023, enabling small businesses to access efficient payment solutions.

## 9.5 Challenges Faced by Islamic Fintech

### 9.5.1 Regulation

Regulatory complexity varies from country to country, making it difficult to implement business models. For example, some fintechs must comply with strict minimum capital requirements.

### 9.5.2 Education and Awareness

According to a Deloitte study, only 30% of Muslims are aware of Islamic financial products, highlighting the need for targeted educational programs.

## 9.6 Outlook for Islamic Fintech

### 9.6.1 Continuous Growth

The Islamic fintech market is expected to grow by 20% annually, reaching a total of $120 billion by 2025, according to Fitch Ratings.

### 9.6.2 Partnerships

Collaborations between fintechs and traditional banks, such as the partnership between **CIMB Islamic Bank** and **BigPay**, foster innovation and improve access to financial services.

### 9.6.3 Integration of New Technologies

The use of artificial intelligence for risk management and blockchain for transparency and security could transform the Islamic finance landscape.

**Dr. Al-Ghamdi** notes that technology is a key driver for the expansion of Islamic finance, particularly with the emergence of fintech solutions that cater to a broader audience.[22]

## 9.7 Interview d'expert: Dr. Ahmad Al-Ghamdi[23]

Dr. Ahmad Al-Ghamdi is a recognized expert in Islamic finance and advisor to several Islamic fintech startups, working at the intersection of technology and ethical finance.

**1. What opportunities do you see for Islamic fintech in the coming years?**

---

[22] Mohammed Al-Ghamdi, *Fintech and Islamic Finance: The Future of Financial Services* (2020, page 112).

[23] Ahmad Al-Ghamdi, Interview conducted on March 7, 2022, in Dubai, United Arab Emirates, during the Global Islamic FinTech Summit.

*« Islamic fintech has enormous potential, especially in high population growth regions like Africa and Southeast Asia. With better financial education and increased awareness of Islamic finance principles, we could see a significant leap in the adoption of these products. The digitalization of Islamic financial services could also facilitate access for unbanked populations, potentially transforming the economic landscape by making these services available to a larger number of people. »*

**2. What major challenges will they need to overcome?**

*« Regulation is an ongoing challenge for Islamic fintech. While many countries are beginning to develop suitable regulatory frameworks, uncertainties remain regarding Sharia compliance and the harmonization of regulations internationally. However, I believe that technological innovation, combined with proactive collaboration between governments and the private sector, can help overcome some of these obstacles. This includes establishing common standards for Islamic fintech products. »*

**3. How do you envision the future of Islamic fintech?**

*« I am confident that within 5 to 10 years, Islamic fintech will be integrated into the very fabric of the global economy. They will play a crucial role in funding sustainable development initiatives, especially in green energy and infrastructure. The rise of responsible and ethical finance aligns with the values of Islamic finance, creating a conducive environment for their expansion. Moreover, with the rise of blockchain technology and*

*smart contracts, we may see significant innovations in Islamic financial products. »*

# 10. Islamic Finance and Financial Markets: Issues and Perspectives

Islamic finance, with its ethical foundations and strict rules regarding *riba* (interest) and *gharar* (excessive uncertainty), has gained an increasingly important place in global financial markets. Islamic financial products—such as *sukuk*, Sharia-compliant investment funds, and Islamic stock indices—offer a credible alternative to conventional finance. Observing this expansion, many experts emphasize its impact and future prospects.

## 10.1 Relationship Between Islamic Finance and Financial Markets

**Sukuk (Islamic bonds):**

The sukuk market has played a key role in the development of Islamic financial markets. Sukuk are structured to comply with the Islamic prohibition of *riba*. By being backed by tangible assets, sukuk bring stability and transparency, while promoting a real-economy orientation that avoids the excesses of speculative finance.[24]

**Islamic Indices:**

Sharia-compliant indices provide investors with an alternative to conventional stocks. They exclude prohibited sectors such as alcohol, tobacco, and gambling. The introduction of Islamic indices has allowed Muslim

---

[24] Mohammad Taqi Usmani, *Islamic Finance: Principles and Practice* (2002, page 76).

investors to participate in stock markets while staying true to their values, thereby fostering a broader integration of Islamic finance principles into the global economy.[25]

## 10.2 Current Challenges of Islamic Finance in Financial Markets

Islamic finance still faces several challenges in establishing itself globally:

**Harmonization of Standards:**

The diversity of interpretations of Sharia principles creates regulatory challenges. The absence of standardized rules sometimes slows down the international expansion of Islamic financial products. The harmonization of international Islamic finance standards is essential to ensure investor confidence and the efficiency of Sharia-compliant financial products.[26]

**Complexity of Financial Products:**

Islamic products are often perceived as more complex, which may discourage some potential investors. However, Muhammad Iqbal points out that this complexity stems from the necessity to avoid *riba* and *gharar* while

[25] Ibrahim Warde, *Islamic Finance in the Global Economy* (2010, page 54).
[26] Habib Ahmed, *Islamic Finance: Theoretical and Practical Perspective* (2010, page 48).

providing alternatives to conventional instruments—yet this has not prevented their rapid adoption.[27]

## 10.3 The Gulf Countries and the Use of Islamic Finance in Financial Markets

The Gulf countries play a central role in the development of Islamic financial markets:

- **Saudi Arabia:** Through *Vision 2030*, Saudi Arabia has heavily invested in sukuk to finance infrastructure projects while strengthening its Islamic financial institutions. According to an Ernst & Young report on Islamic banking, *"Saudi Arabia has emerged as one of the global leaders in Islamic finance, particularly through the increase in sukuk issuance aimed at diversifying its economy."*[28]

- **United Arab Emirates:** Dubai aspires to become the world capital of the Islamic economy. The initiative *Dubai: Capital of the Islamic Economy* seeks to attract Islamic capital and reinforce the role of Islamic finance in global financial markets. According to the *Global Islamic Finance Report 2021* published by Cambridge IFA, the UAE is well positioned to become a central hub not only for sukuk but also for Islamic fintech.[29]

---

[27] Muhammad Iqbal, *Islamic banking: A Modern Approach* (2001, page 112).
[28] Ernst & Young, *World Islamic Banking Competitiveness Report* (2020, page 38).
[29] Cambridge IFA, *Global Islamic Finance Report* (2021, page 60).

## 10.4 Prospects for Islamic Finance in Financial Markets

**Growth of Green Sukuk:** With the growing emphasis on sustainable investment, green sukuk have emerged as a key product. These Sharia-compliant bonds are designed to finance environmentally friendly projects. According to a report by the Islamic Development Bank, green sukuk represent a major opportunity to support sustainable development initiatives in Muslim countries while respecting Islamic principles.[30]

**Islamic Fintech:** Islamic financial technologies open up new opportunities. They provide small businesses and individuals with easier access to Sharia-compliant financial products. According to the *Islamic Fintech Report 2021*, innovation in the Islamic fintech sector could revolutionize access to financial services in emerging economies, particularly in Africa and Southeast Asia.[31]

### Conclusion: Islamic Finance and Evolving Financial Markets

Islamic finance has demonstrated that it can play a central role in global financial markets while addressing the ethical needs of a more sustainable economy. As the world moves toward more responsible models, Islamic

---

[30] Islamic Development Bank, *Sukuk for Sustainability development* (2019, page 24).
[31] Cambridge IFA, Islamic Fintech Report (2021, page 15).

finance has the potential to offer a robust alternative, based on principles of justice and fair risk-sharing.[32]

Islamic finance has demonstrated that it can play a central role in global financial markets while addressing the ethical needs of a more sustainable economy. As the world moves toward more responsible models, Islamic finance has the potential to offer a robust alternative, based on principles of justice and fair risk-sharing.

---

[32] Muhammad S. H. K. Siddiqi, *Islamic Finance: Principles and Practice* (2012, page 219).

## 11. Ethics and Social Responsibility: The Sustainable Core of Islamic Finance

Islamic finance is intrinsically linked to ethics and social justice. Its core principles—such as the prohibition of *riba* (interest) and *gharar* (excessive uncertainty)—ensure that financial transactions remain fair and transparent. *Zakat* (obligatory almsgiving) and the prohibition of investments in immoral sectors further strengthen its social role.

**Examples :**

- **Islamic Development Bank (IsDB):** The IsDB finances infrastructure projects in developing countries—such as the construction of roads, schools, and hospitals—while ensuring that these projects adhere to ethical principles.

- **Islamic microfinance in Indonesia and Bangladesh:** These initiatives utilize contracts such as *Qard Hasan* (interest-free loans) and *Mudarabah* (profit-sharing) to support small businesses, fostering inclusive economic growth.

In a world where social injustice and economic exploitation appear to be growing, Islamic finance emerges as an ethical and responsible solution. Rooted in principles of fairness, risk-sharing, and the prohibition of usury (*riba*), it provides an alternative framework that places human dignity and justice at its core.

Whereas conventional financial systems often prioritize profit maximization at the expense of collective well-being, Islamic finance ensures that every transaction contributes to social balance. This model—anchored in values of solidarity and accountability—directly addresses the challenges of unrestrained capitalism, which in many cases exacerbates global inequalities.

**Future Perspectives:** With the rise of sustainable and responsible finance, Islamic finance is well-positioned to become a benchmark model. Its focus on ethics and social responsibility can serve as an inspiration for conventional systems. Looking ahead, we may witness greater convergence between Islamic finance and global initiatives such as the United Nations Sustainable Development Goals (SDGs), with more active participation in financing green and socially impactful projects.

As the world faces mounting economic, social, and ecological crises, the appeal of more ethical systems is on the rise. With growing demand for transparency, inclusiveness, and fairness in business, Islamic finance has the potential to become a reference model in global discussions on sustainable economics.

# 12. Toward Global Standardization: International Norms and Harmonization in Islamic Finance

Islamic finance is regulated by various bodies such as the **AAOIFI (Accounting and Auditing Organization for Islamic Financial Institutions)** and the **IFSB (Islamic Financial Services Board)**. However, harmonizing practices remains a major challenge, as each country may have its own interpretations of *shariah* rules. Islamic banks also face compatibility issues with international financial regulations such as the **IFRS (International Financial Reporting Standards)**.

**Examples :**

- **AAOIFI Standardization:** AAOIFI has developed specific accounting standards for Islamic finance, which have been adopted in more than 45 countries.

- **Regulation in Malaysia and the Gulf:** Malaysia has adopted a centralized approach with a national *shariah* council to oversee its Islamic banks, whereas Gulf countries operate under more fragmented regulatory frameworks.

Although Islamic finance is expanding rapidly, it suffers from regulatory disparities and a lack of standardization. This fragmentation makes the universal application of Islamic principles difficult, particularly as interpretations vary across regions. Yet, in an increasingly globalized and interconnected world, harmonization of financial practices is not only desirable but necessary. The evolution of Islamic finance toward global norms would not only facilitate integration into the wider financial system but also enhance its attractiveness to international investors.

**Future Perspectives:** The future of Islamic finance will largely depend on regulators' ability to harmonize standards at the global level. Efforts will likely focus on aligning Islamic finance more closely with international standards while still preserving its fundamental principles. Technological innovation may also play a role in facilitating harmonization, especially through standardized digital platforms.

With the rise of global conversations around sustainable finance, Islamic finance could assume a leadership role if concerted efforts are made to unify its principles on an international scale. Initiatives such as AAOIFI standards and the Islamic Financial Services Board (IFSB) guidelines must be strengthened to ensure smooth and standardized growth.

# 13. Regulation and Governance: Challenges and Opportunities for a Robust Framework

Compliance with *shariah* and the independence of *shariah* boards are major issues in the governance of Islamic financial institutions. Unlike conventional banks, Islamic banks must strictly adhere to religious principles, which adds layers of complexity to their operations.

**Examples :**

- **Independent Shariah Boards:** Most Islamic financial institutions are required to have a *shariah* board overseeing financial products and ensuring compliance with Islamic rules. Dubai Islamic Bank and Bank Islam Malaysia are examples of institutions with highly respected boards.

- **Fragmentation Issue:** In some countries, the *shariah* boards of Islamic banks operate independently of each other, leading to inconsistencies in the application of financial principles.

Recent economic crises have exposed the fragility of conventional financial systems, often undermined by speculative practices and insufficient regulation. Islamic finance, with its strict rules prohibiting *riba* (usury/interest) and excessive speculation (*gharar*), offers a potentially more stable framework. However, to become a true alternative, Islamic financial institutions must strengthen both their governance and regulatory mechanisms, particularly in the face of global economic pressures.

**Future Perspectives**: Looking ahead, there could be greater centralization of *shariah* boards, with increased efforts to standardize regulatory processes. Advances in artificial intelligence and blockchain technology may also enhance governance in Islamic institutions by improving transparency and ensuring compliance with *shariah* rules.

With stronger regulation and improved governance, Islamic finance could become a model of resilience in the face of future financial crises. The establishment of international regulators dedicated to Islamic finance would ensure better supervision while maintaining high standards of transparency and accountability.

**Dr. Ahmad Al-Ghamdi**, Interview conducted on March 7, 2022, in Dubai, United Arab Emirates, during the Global Islamic FinTech Summit.

*"One of the most pressing challenges in Islamic finance today is not only compliance with shariah principles but also ensuring that governance structures are transparent, accountable, and resilient. The independence of shariah boards must be preserved, but at the same time, coordination is essential to avoid fragmentation across different jurisdictions. In my view, technology will be the great equalizer. Blockchain, for instance, can provide immutable records of compliance, while artificial intelligence can monitor transactions in real time to detect deviations from shariah. If we succeed in marrying governance, technology, and shariah compliance, Islamic finance will not just be an alternative system—it could*

*become a benchmark for ethical and resilient finance globally."*

## 14. The Impact of Islamic Finance on the Green Economy: A Catalyst for Sustainable Development

By its ethical nature, Islamic finance is well-suited to the green economy. The prohibition of investments in harmful sectors (such as alcohol and gambling) and its promotion of the *maslaha* (public good) are directly aligned with the principles of environmental sustainability.

**Examples :**

- **Green Sukuk:** In Indonesia, Green Sukuk have been used to finance renewable energy projects such as solar power plants and hydroelectric dams. This model provides a concrete example of how Islamic finance can contribute to the green economy.

- **Green Islamic Banks:** Initiatives such as the Green Islamic Bank project in Malaysia aim to finance environmentally friendly projects while generating returns in compliance with *shariah.*

Faced with climate challenges, the world urgently needs a new economic paradigm that prioritizes environmentally responsible development. Islamic finance, with its ban on harmful industries and its promotion of ethical investment, provides a viable solution. It encourages investments in sustainable sectors, such as renewable energy, while fostering the responsible use of resources.

**Future Perspectives**: In the coming decades, Islamic finance could play an increasingly significant role in funding environmentally focused projects. The rise of Green Sukuk and sustainable investments will create synergies between Islamic finance and global initiatives to combat climate change.

In the coming decades, Islamic finance could play an increasingly significant role in funding environmentally focused projects. The rise of Green Sukuk and sustainable investments will create synergies between Islamic finance and global initiatives to combat climate change.

**Dr. Mohamad A. El-Gamal**, Interview conducted on September 29, 2021, in Houston, Texas, United States, following a conference at Rice University on Islamic Economics.

*"Islamic finance is uniquely positioned to support the transition toward a green economy. Its ethical foundations—avoiding harmful industries and prioritizing projects that benefit society—are in natural harmony with the principles of environmental sustainability. The example of Green Sukuk in Indonesia is just the beginning; we are likely to see more such instruments being deployed globally. What excites me most is the potential for convergence between Islamic finance and ESG standards. If properly aligned, this could unlock massive flows of capital into renewable energy, sustainable agriculture, and ecological infrastructure. In this sense, Islamic finance does not just complement the global sustainability agenda—it can actually lead it, offering a moral and ethical compass for the financial system of the future."*

# 15. Education and Training: Keys to the Growth of Islamic Finance

Islamic finance remains a misunderstood field, even in countries where it is actively practiced. Efforts to train qualified professionals and educate the general public about its principles and benefits are crucial for its sustainable growth.

**Examples :**

- **Academic Programs:** Many universities, such as Durham University in the United Kingdom and INCEIF (International Centre for Education in Islamic Finance) in Malaysia, offer specialized programs in Islamic finance.

- **Professional Certifications:** Certifications such as those offered by AAOIFI (Accounting and Auditing Organization for Islamic Financial Institutions) or IFQ (Islamic Finance Qualification) enable professionals to acquire recognized expertise in the field.

The growth of Islamic finance cannot take place without a massive educational effort. Many economic stakeholders, particularly in emerging economies, still do not fully understand the nuances of this financial system. It is essential to train not only industry professionals but also investors and consumers, in order to make Islamic financial products more accessible and better understood.

**Future Perspectives**: In the future, with the rise of fintech and the globalization of Islamic finance, the demand for specialized training in Islamic finance will increase significantly. Educational technologies such as e-learning platforms and virtual reality could play a pivotal role in disseminating knowledge, making training more accessible to an international audience.

The development of academic programs, professional certifications, and online educational initiatives could revolutionize the global adoption of Islamic finance. To ensure widespread adoption, Islamic financial institutions, in collaboration with universities and regulators, must invest heavily in education.

**Ahmad Al-Ghamdi**, Interview conducted on March 7, 2022, in Dubai, United Arab Emirates, during the Global Islamic FinTech Summit:

*"Education is the backbone of Islamic finance. Without awareness and training, even the most innovative products will remain underutilized. We need a new generation of professionals who understand both classical shariah principles and modern financial instruments. Universities, regulators, and industry leaders must work hand in hand to create strong academic foundations and professional training programs. With the rise of fintech, the learning process can be transformed—digital platforms, online certifications, and even AI-driven simulations will allow broader access to knowledge. In my view, the countries and institutions that invest seriously in education will become the true leaders of the Islamic finance industry in the decades ahead.*

# 16. Resilience in the Face of COVID-19: Lessons and Adaptations of Islamic Financial Systems

The COVID-19 crisis posed unprecedented challenges to the global economy, yet Islamic banks demonstrated a certain degree of resilience due to their ethical practices and aversion to excessive risk.

**Examples :**

- **Response of Islamic Banks:** In the Middle East, several Islamic banks implemented moratoriums on debt repayments to help clients cope with the crisis. Qatar Islamic Bank, for instance, granted relief to thousands of small businesses.

- **Ethical Investments:** Islamic finance, with its risk-sharing model, proved more stable in the face of financial market volatility during the pandemic.

The COVID-19 pandemic underscored the importance of a resilient financial system capable of supporting the real economy in times of crisis. Islamic finance, with its emphasis on real economic activity and rejection of speculative excesses, demonstrated remarkable robustness against global economic shocks. Contracts based on risk-sharing, such as **Mudarabah** and **Musharakah**, allowed for a fairer distribution of losses and relative stability.

**Future Perspectives:** Looking ahead, the lessons drawn from the pandemic will reinforce the Islamic finance model, particularly regarding its ability to support the real economy. Contracts like **Mudarabah** and **Musharakah**, which share both profits and losses, could become increasingly attractive in a post-pandemic world where stability and resilience are in high demand.

In a post-pandemic global landscape, Islamic finance could establish itself as a model of resilience. By strengthening its mechanisms of economic solidarity and adapting its products to meet the needs of SMEs and entrepreneurs, it has the potential to become a key driver in the global economic recovery.

**Mohammad Usman**, Interview conducted on August 18, 2017, in Lagos, Nigeria, during the African Islamic Finance Forum:

*"The COVID-19 crisis highlighted an essential truth: financial systems anchored in ethics and real economic activity are more resilient than those fueled by speculation. Islamic finance, with its emphasis on risk-sharing and prohibition of excessive uncertainty, has shown that it can protect both institutions and clients during shocks. The relief measures implemented by Islamic banks—such as debt moratoriums—were not just financial decisions but moral imperatives. Moving forward, I believe that Mudarabah and Musharakah will not only serve as financial instruments but as frameworks for rebuilding trust and stability in post-pandemic economies."*

# 17. Conclusion

Islamic finance is emerging as an indispensable tool to address contemporary economic challenges, offering ethical and sustainable solutions in a world often marked by financial crises and growing inequalities. Throughout this exploration, we have highlighted its core principles, its differences from conventional finance, as well as its concrete applications across various economic sectors.

Islamic contracts such as **Mudarabah** and **Musharakah** illustrate a collaborative approach to investment that fosters entrepreneurship and innovation while ensuring equitable risk-sharing. Moreover, case studies from different regions, including Sub-Saharan Africa, demonstrate how Islamic finance can stimulate local economic development while respecting societal values.

The rise of **Islamic fintechs** further reinforces this dynamic by making financial services more accessible and integrating innovative business models. This is particularly relevant in emerging markets, where financial inclusion is crucial for economic growth.

By addressing both challenges and opportunities, it becomes clear that Islamic finance is not merely an alternative to conventional financial systems. On the contrary, it positions itself as a **strategic lever for sustainable development, green financing, and responsible investment**—all essential elements for a prosperous economic future.

Finally, in an increasingly uncertain global context, Islamic finance offers a beacon of hope. Its approach, grounded in ethics and social justice, makes it a well-suited solution for building resilient and inclusive financial systems. By integrating these principles into global economic policies, we may aspire not only to overcome current challenges but also to construct a future where prosperity is shared and sustainable.

In sum, Islamic finance is far more than a financial system: it is a **response to current crises** and a **catalyst for inclusive and sustainable global growth**. It represents a promising path to explore for all who aspire to balanced and ethical economic development.

# 18. Annex – Glossary of Islamic and Financial Terms

This glossary serves as a reference tool to help readers better understand specific terms related to Islamic finance. It can also be complemented by concrete examples or illustrations of each concept to further enrich the reader's experience.

## 1. A

**Agar**: A deferred payment sales contract in which the seller finances the purchase, and the buyer repays the cost through multiple installments.

**Akhlaq**: Ethics or morality; a foundational concept in Islamic finance that ensures fairness, integrity, and responsibility in transactions.

## 2. B

**Bai** (Bay'): A general term for sale. It encompasses various forms of sales contracts under Islamic law.

**Bai' Salam**: A forward sale contract in which payment is made in advance, while the delivery of goods occurs at a later date.

## 3. F

**Fatwa**: A legal opinion or ruling issued by a qualified Sharia scholar on a specific question or matter.

**Fiqh**: Islamic jurisprudence—the understanding, interpretation, and application of Islamic laws, including those related to finance.

**Crowdfunding**: A financing model where a project or enterprise is funded by small contributions from a large number of individuals.

**4. G**

**Gharar**: Uncertainty, ambiguity, or excessive risk in a contract; strictly prohibited in Islamic finance.

**Gharar Mukhafaf**: Uncertainty, ambiguity, or excessive risk in a contract; strictly prohibited in Islamic finance.

**5. I**

**Ijara**: A leasing contract in which the lessor retains ownership of the asset, and the lessee pays rent for its use.

**Ijara Wa Iqtina**: A lease-to-own contract where the lessee has the option to acquire ownership of the asset at the end of the lease term.

**Istisna**: A contract for manufacturing or construction in which payments may be made in stages, with delivery of the finished product or project at a future date.

**6. M**

**Mudarabah**: An investment partnership in which one party provides the capital while the other manages the investment; profits are shared according to a pre-agreed ratio, while losses are borne solely by the capital provider.

**Musharakah**: A joint partnership where all parties contribute capital and share profits and losses according to their respective equity stakes.

**7. Q**

**Qard Hasan**: A joint partnership where all parties contribute capital and share profits and losses according to their respective equity stakes.

**8. R**

**Riba**: Usury or interest; strictly prohibited in Islamic finance as it represents unjust and exploitative gain.

**9. S**

**Sukuk**: Islamic bonds that represent ownership in a tangible asset, project, or investment, structured in accordance with Sharia principles.

**Shariah**: Islamic law, encompassing all aspects of Muslim life, including financial transactions, and ensuring compliance with ethical and religious principles.

**Takaful**: Islamic law, encompassing all aspects of Muslim life, including financial transactions, and ensuring compliance with ethical and religious principles.

## 10. W

**Wakalah**: An agency contract in which one party authorizes another to act on their behalf in specific matters.

# 19. Annex – Glossary of Keys Terms

- **Islamic Finance**

A financial system compliant with Sharia, prohibiting riba (usury/interest) and based on ethical principles such as social justice and risk-sharing.

- **Riba**

Usury or interest, strictly prohibited in Islamic finance. It refers to any form of excessive or unjust gain in financial transactions.

- **Mudarabah**

A partnership contract in which one party (the financier) provides capital, while the other (the entrepreneur) provides effort and expertise. Profits are shared according to a pre-agreed ratio, while losses are borne solely by the financier.

- **Musharakah**

An investment partnership where all parties contribute capital and share profits and losses proportionally to their investment.

- **Takaful**

Islamic insurance based on the principle of mutual assistance, in which participants contribute to a common fund to protect each other against losses.

- **Zakat**

A mandatory charitable contribution in Islam, representing a fixed percentage of an individual's wealth, intended to assist those in need and support social causes.

- **Sukuk**

Islamic financial instruments, often compared to bonds, representing ownership in a specific asset or project, generating a Sharia-compliant return.

- **Shariah**

The body of Islamic law governing the behavior of Muslims, including economic and financial rules.

- **Mudharabah mutaqa'id**

A type of Mudarabah where client deposits in a financial institution are invested, and profits generated are shared with depositors.

- **Islamic Microfinance**

Financial services provided to low-income populations in compliance with Islamic principles, often through small, interest-free loans.

- **Social and Solidarity Economy**

  An economic approach emphasizing social and environmental impact, reflecting the values of justice and equity found in Islamic finance.

- **Shared Risk**

  A central concept in Islamic finance where all parties in a transaction share financial risk, promoting fairer business relationships.

- **Akhlaq**

  A set of ethical and moral principles guiding individual behavior, particularly in commercial transactions.

- **Fiqh**

  The study and interpretation of Islamic laws, especially as they pertain to finance and commercial transactions.

- **Gharar**

  Uncertainty or ambiguity in contracts, prohibited in Islamic finance as it can lead to unfair or unjust transactions.

- **Halal**

  That which is permitted or lawful under Islamic law, particularly in the context of consumption and financial transactions.

- **Haram**

That which is forbidden by Islamic law, including interest (riba) and certain forms of gambling.

- **Islamic Banking**

A banking system operating under Islamic finance principles, avoiding interest and favoring Sharia-compliant investments.

- **Fintech Islamique**

The use of technology to provide Sharia-compliant financial services, facilitating broader access to Islamic finance.

# 20. Annex – Resources and Further Reading

### 1. Books


- The Stability of Islamic Finance (2011). Par Askari, H, Iqbal, Z., Krichene, N. et Mirakhor, A.

- Islamic Finance: Law, Economic and Practice (2006). Par Mahmoud A. El-Gamal.


### 2. Academic Articles


- Iqbal, Z., & Mirakhor, A. (2011). "Financial Stability and Islamic Finance." Journal of Financial Stability.

- Usmani, M. T. (2002). "Islamic Finance: Principles and Practice." Journal of Islamic Banking and Finance.

- Al-Ghamdi, A. (2020). "The Role of Fintech in Islamic Finance." International Journal of Islamic Finance.


### 3. Reports


- Global Islamic Finance Report (GIFR) (2022). "Islamic Finance Industry Trends and Developments."

- World Bank Report (2021). "Islamic Finance: A Global Perspective."

## 4. Conferences and Cass Studies

- Proceedings of the International Conference on Islamic Finance and Economics.

- **9th International Conference on Islamic Finance in Turkey (ICIF):** Held in December 2023 in Istanbul, covering topics such as Shariah auditing, Islamic financial technology, and innovations in Islamic finance.

- **11th International Conference on Islamic Banking, Accounting, and Finance (IBAF):** Scheduled for November 2024, organized by the Universiti Sains Islam Malaysia (USIM), focusing on the integration of artificial intelligence in Islamic banking and finance.

## 5. Web Sites

- **Islamic Financial Services Board (IFSB) -** www.ifsb.org
  An organization that promotes standards and guidelines for the Islamic finance sector.
- **Accounting and Auditing Organization for Islamic Financial Institutions (AAOIFI) -** www.aaoifi.com
  An organization that promotes standards and guidelines for the Islamic finance sector.

# 21. Bibliography – Academic References and Case Studies

**Quranic Verses**

1. Al-Baqarah (2 :188).
2. Al-Anfal (8 : 27).
3. Al-Baqarah (2 : 275).

**Books**

1. Ahmed, Habib. *Islamic Finance: Theoretical and Practical Perspectives*. 2010. Page 48.
2. Al-Ghamdi, Mohammed. *Fintech and Islamic Finance: The Future of Financial Services*. 2020. Page 112.
3. El-Gamal, Mahmoud. *Islamic Finance*. 2006. Page 40.
4. Gueranger, François. *Finance Islamique : Une Illustration De La Finance Éthique*. 2009. Page 72.
5. Iqbal, Muhammad. *Islamic Banking: A Modern Approach*. 2001. Page 112.
6. Iqbal, Zamir et Mirakhor, Abbas. *An Introduction to Islamic Finance: Theory and Practice*. John Wiley & Sons, 2011.
7. Iqbal, Zamir et Mirakhor, Abbas. *The Role of Islamic Finance in Economic Development*. *Islamic Economic Studies*, vol. 21, no. 2, 2013, pp. 15-29.
8. Mzid, Wadi. *La finance islamique : principes fondamentaux et apports potentiels dans le financement de la croissance et du développement*. 2011. Page 56.
9. Siddiqi, Muhammad S. H. K. *Islamic Finance: Principles and Practice*. 2012. Page 219.

10. Usmani, Muhammad Taqi. *An Introduction to Islamic Finance*. Kluwer Law International, 2002.
11. Usmani, Muhammad Taqi. *Islamic Finance: Principles and Practice*. 2002. Page 76.
12. Usmani, Muhammad Taqi. *Islamic Finance: Principles and Practice*. 2011. Page 45.
13. Visser, Hans. *Islamic Finance : Principles and Practice*. 2009, Page 10.
14. Warde, Ibrahim. *Islamic Finance in the Global Economy*. 2010. Page 54.

## Academic Articles

1. Khan, M. Fahim. "Islamic Finance: An Overview." *Journal of Islamic Finance*, vol. 1, no. 1, 2012, pp. 1-10.
2. Ahmed, Habib. "Islamic Finance: The Challenge of the 21st Century." *Journal of Islamic Economics, Banking and Finance*, vol. 6, no. 1, 2010, pp. 1-20.
3. Khan Shahrukh Rafi. "An Economic Analysis of a PLS Model for the Financial Sector." *Pakistan Journal of Applied Economics*, vol. 3, no. 2, 1984, pp. 89-105.

## Raports and Markets Astudies

1. Ernst & Young. *World Islamic Banking Competitiveness Report*, 2020, Page 38.
2. Cambridge IFA. *Global Islamic Finance Report*, 2021, Page 60.
3. Cambridge IFA. *Islamic Fintech Report*, 2021, Page 15.
4. Islamic Development Bank. *Sukuk for Sustainable Development*, 2021, Page 24.

**Case Studiesd**

1. Hassan, Mohamad and Lewis, Mark K. "Islamic Banking: The New Norm." *Banking and Finance Review*, vol. 2, no. 1, 2017, pp. 55-72.
2. Obaidullah, Muhammad. "Islamic Microfinance: A Better Solution for Poverty Alleviation?" *Journal of Islamic Economics, Banking and Finance*, vol. 6, no. 1, 2010, pp. 21-36.

**Interviews**

1. Ahmad Al-Ghamdi, Interview conducted on March 7, 2022, in Dubai, United Arab Emirates, during the Global Islamic FinTech Summit.
2. Muhammad Imran Ashraf Usmani, Interview conducted on January 25, 2022, in Karachi, Pakistan, during the Islamic finance conference organized by Dar Al Sharia.
3. Aisha Yousuf, Interview conducted on April 22, 2019, in Kuala Lumpur, Malaysia, during the International Islamic Finance Congress.
4. Abbas Mirakhor, Interview conducted on June 10, 2022, in Washington, D.C., United States, during a symposium organized by the Islamic Development Bank (IDB).
5. Mohammad Usman, Interview conducted on August 18, 2017, in Lagos, Nigeria, during the African Islamic Finance Forum.
6. Mohamad A. El-Gamal, Interview conducted on September 29, 2021, in Houston, Texas, United States, after a lecture at Rice University on Islamic economics.

## Online Resources

1. Islamic Finance News (IFN). *Islamic Finance News Portal*. Available at *www.islamicfinancenews.com.*
2. AAOIFI. *Accounting and Auditing Organization for Islamic Financial Institutions*. Available at *www.aaoifi.com.*

# TABLE OF CONTENTS

## Structures éditoriales du groupe L'Harmattan

**L'Harmattan Italie**
Via degli Artisti, 15
10124 Torino
harmattan.italia@gmail.com

**L'Harmattan Hongrie**
Kossuth l. u. 14-16.
1053 Budapest
harmattan@harmattan.hu

**L'Harmattan Sénégal**
10 VDN SICAP AMITIE 3
BP 45034 Dakar-Fann
direction@senharmattan.com

**L'Harmattan Cameroun**
Tsinga/Derrière polyclinique FECAFOOT
BP 11486 Yaoundé
Jacques.koukam@harmattan.fr

**L'Harmattan Burkina Faso**
Villa 281, secteur 23 623, rue 14.32
Ouagadougou
zagbie@outlook.fr

**L'Harmattan Guinée**
Almamya, rue KA 028 OKB Agency
BP 3470 Conakry
harmattanguinee@yahoo.fr

**L'Harmattan RDC**
185, avenue Nyangwe
Commune de Lingwala – Kinshasa
matangilamusadila@yahoo.fr

**L'Harmattan Congo**
219, avenue Nelson Mandela
BP 2874 Brazzaville
deunovmikhael@gmail.com

**L'Harmattan Mali**
Immeuble Mgr Jean Marie Cissé
Aci Hamadallaye
BP 145 Bamako
syllaka@yahoo.fr

**L'Harmattan Togo**
Djidjole – Maison Amela
face EPP BATOME
02 BP 20680 Lomé
didieramela11@gmail.com

**L'Harmattan Côte d'Ivoire**
Résidence Karl – Cité des Arts
Abidjan-Cocody
03 BP 1588 Abidjan
harmattan.ivoire@gmail.com

**L'Harmattan Bénin**
Rue 604, (Immeuble à l'entrée
de la rue UCAO- Cite de Saint-Jean)
Cotonou
stepcorpus@gmail.com

## Nos librairies en France

**Librairie internationale**
16, rue des Écoles
75005 Paris
librairie.internationale@harmattan.fr
01 40 46 79 11
www.librairieharmattan.com

**Librairie des savoirs**
21, rue des Écoles
75005 Paris
librairie.sh@harmattan.fr
01 46 34 13 71
www.librairieharmattansh.com

www.ingramcontent.com/pod-product-compliance
Lightning Source LLC
LaVergne TN
LVHW051400061026
849535LV00009B/3279
* 9 7 8 2 3 3 6 5 8 7 7 8 3 *